Natu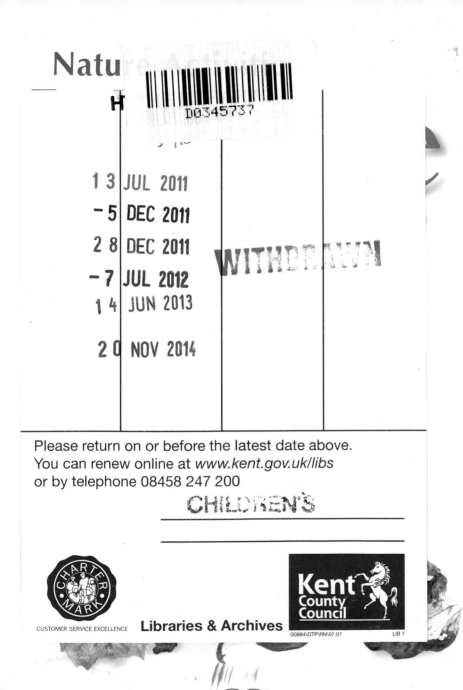

D0345737

1 3 JUL 2011
- 5 DEC 2011
2 8 DEC 2011
- 7 JUL 2012
1 4 JUN 2013

2 0 NOV 2014

WITHDRAWN

Please return on or before the latest date above.
You can renew online at *www.kent.gov.uk/libs*
or by telephone 08458 247 200

CHILDREN'S

DK

LONDON, NEW YORK,
MELBOURNE, MUNICH, AND DELHI

Produced for Dorling Kindersley Ltd by
Cooling Brown Ltd:
Creative Director Arthur Brown
Editor Kesta Desmond
Designers Tish Jones, Elaine Hewson

For Dorling Kindersley Ltd:
Senior Editor Shaila Brown
Senior Art Editor Stefan Podhorodecki
Managing Editor Linda Esposito
Managing Art Editor
Diane Thistlethwaite
Publishing Managers
Caroline Buckingham, Andrew Macintyre
Jacket Designer Neal Cobourne
Jacket Copywriter Adam Powley
Jacket Editor Mariza O'Keefe
Publishing Director Laura Buller
Production Controller Erica Rosen
Picture Researcher Frances Vargo
DK Picture Library Claire Bowers,
Rose Horridge
DTP Designer Siu Chan
Photography Dave King
Consultant Kim Bryan

First published in Great Britain in 2006
by Dorling Kindersley Limited,
80 Strand, London WC2R 0RL
Copyright © 2006 Dorling Kindersley Limited
A Penguin Company

07 08 09 10 9 8 7 6 5 4 3

A CIP catalogue for this book
is available from the British Library.
ISBN-13: 978-1-40531-036-9

Colour reproduction by Colourscan, Singapore
Printed in China by L. Rex Printing Co., Ltd.

**Discover more at
www.dk.com**

BE SAFE! IMPORTANT NOTE TO PARENTS
Some of the activities in this book require adult supervision.
Symbols are used to indicate where an activity must only be
done with the help of an adult. An "Important" box gives
further information about any risks involved and appropriate
safety precautions to take. Please carefully check which activities
require adult supervision and supervise your child where indicated.

Activities shown with this symbol must only be
done with the help of an adult.

Take extra care when doing this activity.

IMPORTANT
Provides safety information and indicates whether an activity can be messy. Follow the guidance notes on those activities that are messy and should be carried out only in suitable places.

Always ensure that your child follows
instructions carefully. The author and
the publisher cannot take responsibility
for any accident or injury that occurs
because the reader has not followed
the instructions properly and will not
be responsible for any loss or damage
allegedly arising from any of the
activities in this book.

Contents

Remember!
Show respect to wild creatures and make sure you don't disturb animals' environments.

CHILDREN – BE SAFE!
READ THIS BEFORE STARTING ANY ACTIVITIES!

1 Tell an adult before you do any of the activities in this book as you may need an adult to supervise the activity.

2 Pay attention to the following symbols:

⚠ Take extra care with an activity.

⚠ You need an adult to help you with an activity.

3 Read the "Important" boxes – these provide safety information and let you know which activities may be messy and should only be carried out in suitable places.

4 Follow the instructions carefully.

The world of nature

We are surrounded by an amazing world of nature – an incredible array of animals, plants, and other living things that live in gardens, woodlands, meadows, lakes, rivers, and a host of other places. It doesn't matter whether you live in a city, town, or in the countryside, you can find out lots about this magical world by becoming a nature ranger. It's fun and fascinating, and details of how to do it can be found in the pages that follow.

Harsh conditions
Even the harshest conditions do not deter some organisms. These orange lichens – a combination of fungus and alga – have colonized bare rocks on a windy cliff top.

Plant competitors
Providing it's not too cold, plants grow wherever there is water and light. Plants, unlike animals, do not move around, and they make their own food using sunlight energy. So light is essential for survival, and plants, such as these bluebells in a woodland clearing, compete with their neighbours to make sure they get access to it.

PLANET EARTH

View from space ▲
Taken by a satellite, this photo shows blue oceans, green landmasses, and polar ice.

As far as we know, Earth is the only planet with living organisms. They live in its air, water, on land, and in soil. Earth has water that is vital for life. It has an atmosphere that contains essential oxygen. Its temperatures are neither too hot nor too cold. Earth also supports plants, which harness sunlight to provide an energy source for themselves and all other organisms.

STUDYING NATURE

Scientists who study the living world are called biologists. The two main branches of biology are zoology (the study of animals) and botany (the study of plants). But there are lots of other branches, too. While some biologists work in laboratories, others do more of their research outdoors. They include ecologists, who investigate how living things interact with their surroundings.

◄ Puffin researcher
A Norwegian ecologist measures a puffin chick, called a puffling. This is part of his research into Atlantic puffin populations in their cliff-top nesting sites.

Active animals

From termites to tigers, animals form the largest and most varied group of living things. Animals feed on plants or other animals. To find food they move actively and use their senses, just like this grizzly bear, which has caught a migrating salmon.

Essential equipment

Nature ranging is something that might take a few minutes or a whole day. But you can often make the experience more interesting by having the right equipment at the right time. For example, there's nothing more frustrating than spotting a distant bird or mammal that you cannot identify because you haven't got a pair of binoculars.

NATURE RANGER'S CODE

When you are nature ranging, do not harm any wildlife or yourself. Always follow these five rules:

- Don't touch any animal or fungus with your bare hands unless you know it is harmless.
- Don't pick wild flowers. You can draw or photograph them instead.
- If you take any animals, return them to their homes after studying them.
- If you move logs or rocks, return them carefully to their original position.
- In the countryside, always close any gates and keep to footpaths.

FIELD KIT

Here you can see some useful nature-ranging equipment. Use this field kit to spot, record, and collect wildlife. You won't need to take all these items with you at the same time. Sometimes you may need other equipment such as dip nets (see opposite).

To take photos

To observe from afar

Camera

Binoculars

Notebook, pen, coloured pencils

Magnifying glass

To take notes and sketch

To see tiny creatures

Tweezers

To pick up specimens

Torch

To see at night

Self-seal plastic bags

For samples

Small plastic box with lid

For living specimens

Nature expedition

It's often more fun, and safer, to go on a nature expedition with some friends. You can compare notes and share information about what you find. These children are doing some pond dipping in search of freshwater animals. They are using dip nets and buckets.

ON SCREEN

Got a digital camera and a computer? Then take pictures of the wildlife you find when you go nature ranging. You can store these on your computer. It's a great way to keep a record of your expeditions.

Pond skater ▶
You can enlarge images of the creatures you photograph. This is an image of a pond skater, an insect that walks over the surface of ponds.

WHERE TO LOOK

- In gardens – for bird visitors that feed on worms, beetles, or at a bird table.
- In woodland trees and bushes – for songbirds, woodpeckers, and owls.
- Near the coast – for gulls and terns.
- On seashores – for wading birds.
- On rivers and lakes – for waterfowl, herons, and kingfishers.
- In mountainous areas and open country – for birds of prey.

Animals in action

Whether you are lying on a beach, exploring in a wood, or cleaning out a cellar, in all these places – and many more – you should see animals in action. Remember, however, some animals live their lives hidden from our gaze – unless we make a special effort to look for them. But others, especially birds, are easily seen, even in cities. Find out how to watch birds and record what you see.

CREATE A NATURE DIARY

What better way to record your nature-ranging activities than to create a nature diary. You can make notes about the animals that you see, where and when you saw them, and what they were doing. Make drawings and take photographs to illustrate your diary, and stick in feathers, fur, and any other items that provide evidence of animals in action. Don't forget to record the plants and fungi that you see as well!

Keep a week by week record of what you see

1st July
Birds on backgarden feeder eating peanuts

Birdwatching

Whether you have a few minutes to spare, or all day, you can become a birdwatcher. Identifying birds may be a bit frustrating at first, but be patient. In time – with the help of your binoculars and bird guide – you'll be able to recognize species not just by their shape, size, and colouring, but also by the way they move and behave.

SUNBATHERS

If you live or visit somewhere that has long, warm summers you will probably see lizards sunbathing on walls or rocks in the early morning sun. This is because the body temperature of lizards and other reptiles varies with outside temperature, so they need to reach a certain body temperature to become active enough to search for food.

Spiny footed lizard sunbathing on a rock

WHAT YOU WILL NEED

- Notebook
- Pencil
- Binoculars
- Camera
- Bird identification guide

ANIMAL VARIETY

Below are the main animal groups. The first five groups are vertebrates – animals with backbones. But the sixth – invertebrates – includes many more species than vertebrates.

Mammals ▶
These warm-blooded animals have hairy bodies, feed their young on milk, and include bats, cats, deer, horses, and, of course, you.

Field mouse

Birds ▶
Also warm-blooded, birds have feathers, they can fly, and they lay eggs from which young hatch. They feed using toothless beaks.

Herring gull

Reptiles ▶
Snakes, lizards, turtles, and crocodiles are all reptiles – animals that lay eggs, have a scaly skin, and need external warmth to become active.

Grass snake

Amphibians ▶
Creatures, such as frogs, toads, salamanders, and newts, live both in water and on land. They are moist-skinned, cold-blooded animals.

Frog

Stickleback

Fish ▶
These powerful swimmers with streamlined bodies, slippery scales, and gills for breathing, are perfectly adapted for life in freshwater or in the sea.

Invertebrates ▶
Animals that lack backbones, such as molluscs, worms, crustaceans, and insects, are known as invertebrates.

Grasshopper

Creepy crawlies, worms, and slugs

You are sure to come across creepy crawlies, worms, slugs, and their relatives while nature ranging. Creepy crawlies include insects and other animals, such as centipedes, spiders, and scorpions, with tough outer skeletons and jointed legs. Worms include earthworms and, from the seaside, ragworms, while slug relatives include snails. Although some of these groups are distantly related they are all described as invertebrates – animals that lack a backbone. Try making this trap to see which invertebrates live nearby.

WHAT YOU WILL NEED

- Grapefruit
- Chopping board
- Knife
- Spoon
- Notebook and/or digital camera
- Pencil
- Paintbrush
- Small plastic container

Ask an adult to help you cut the grapefruit.

1 **Take the grapefruit** and ask an adult to cut it in half. Scoop out the flesh using the spoon (the flesh can be put aside and eaten later).

3 **The next morning**, turn over the grapefruit skins to see what you have trapped. Brush animals into the plastic container and try to identify them. Slugs, snails, woodlice, and beetles are common visitors. Note down, or photograph, what you have found.

A garden slug is lured into the trap

2 **In the evening**, put the grapefruit skins, hollow surface down, on the soil in two different, sheltered locations in your garden. Leave them out overnight. Hopefully, creepy crawlies, slugs, and other small animals will take refuge under the juicy "umbrella".

EARTHWORM GARDENERS

To be healthy and good for plant growth, soil needs earthworms. These invertebrates feed on soil, digesting its nutrients. When they burrow through the ground, they mix the soil layers, bringing important substances to the top. Earthworms also carry dead matter down from the surface. You'll see these natural gardeners if you dig into soil, or when they come to the surface on warm, moist nights.

◄ Worm burrows
The burrows made by earthworms let the soil "breathe", allowing plant roots to get oxygen. They also help rainwater to drain away so soil does not get waterlogged.

INVERTEBRATE GUIDE

Here is a quick visual guide to some of the small creatures you might come across when you are nature ranging. You can also use the guide at the front of this book. This shows all the main animal groups.

Insects ►
With six jointed legs, and a body made of three parts, insects are the most numerous of all animals. They include beetles, wasps, and butterflies.

Ground beetle

Centipedes ►
Fast-running with long, flat bodies, these many-legged hunters kill prey using two poisonous fang-like claws.

Woodland centipede

Crustaceans ►
Crabs and other crustaceans have hard outer skeletons and several pairs of jointed legs. Most live in water, but a few, such as woodlice, live on land.

Hermit crab

Spiders ►
With a body divided into two sections, and four pairs of legs, spiders are carnivores with fangs that release deadly poison into their prey.

House spider

Scorpions ►
Living in warmer countries, these eight-legged spider relatives catch prey with their claws. Then they paralyse it with the poisonous sting at the end of their bendy "tail".

Imperial scorpion

Worms ►
Various groups of animals that have a long, soft, legless body are referred to as worms. They include earthworms, leeches, ragworms, and flatworms.

Ragworm

Molluscs ►
Snails, slugs, and other molluscs have a soft body, often protected by a hard shell. Most are slow-moving but one group, squid and octopuses, are fast-moving.

Banded snail

HANDY TIP

After you have studied and identified small creatures, always return them to where you found them.

WHAT YOU WILL NEED

- Four garden canes around 1.5 m (5 ft) long (for the uprights)
- Four garden canes around 1 m (3 ft) long (for the cross-bars)
- String
- Scissors
- Garden netting (such as that used by gardeners to protect soft fruit from birds)
- Twigs, leaves, and ferns
- Binoculars or camera
- Notebook and pencil

Wildlife detective

Most birds and mammals will generally make a rapid escape if they sense the presence of a human. So, to be able to watch and photograph creatures at close range, you need to use some tricks to conceal yourself. One of the best ways of doing this is to build a hide using leaves and netting. Once you're inside the hide, nearby creatures won't know you're there, and will behave completely naturally.

1 **Pick a suitable** place for the hide, for example, in a garden or wood. Push the long canes into the ground to form a square. Each side should be just under 1 m (3 ft), which is the length of the cross-bars.

2 **Using string**, tie one of the cross-bars to two of the upright long canes, just below the top of those canes. Repeat with the other cross-bar canes to form a square around the top of the uprights.

3 **Drape the netting** over the canes. Decide on the entry point to the hide – probably near to trees or shrubs. Insert fallen leaves, twigs, and ferns into the netting to camouflage the hide.

LOW PROFILE

This is a quick alternative to building a hide. Collect some leafy branches or fern fronds, lie on the ground, and use them to cover yourself. With a low profile, leafy camouflage, and by staying still, you can watch animals without them noticing, even when you are very close.

◄ **Undercover**
A covering of leaves and branches breaks up the outline of your body so it is much less obvious to passing animals. You could also use brown and green face paint to disguise yourself.

Birds will come very close because they cannot see you

HANDY TIP

Don't make any unnecessary noises in the hide — even small sounds will frighten animals away.

4 **Get inside the hide**, and clear several small bits of camouflage so you can see out at eye level. Keep quiet, be patient, and wait for mammals and birds to arrive. Use your binoculars or camera to get a close-up view, and make a note of what you see.

Leaves mask the outline of the hide, making it "invisible"

SCENT AND WIND

Most land mammals have a very keen sense of smell. If you are watching mammals, check the wind direction. Make sure that any breeze or wind is blowing into your face. If the wind is blowing in the opposite direction, your scent will be carried towards the animal and may frighten it away.

◀ **Weasel**
This small predator raises its snout to sniff the air. It will detect the smell of humans as well as that of prey.

Trails and traces

Whether active at night or during the day, many wild animals are creatures of habit. They follow the same trails and pathways whenever they go in search of food. If you discover a trail, you may get clues as to the animal's identity from the size of the trail or from any traces that the passing animal has left behind, such as a scrap of fur. Even animals that have visited an area only once may accidentally deposit vital evidence. It's up to you to spot these trails and traces.

Animal runways
Some mammals, including this nocturnal badger, follow regular paths that can wear away grass and undergrowth, leaving a visible path or runway.

TRACKING ANIMALS

At one time, the only way to study the movement and behaviour of an animal was to follow it. Today, biologists can track animals by fitting them with radio collars. These send out radio signals, which are picked up by aerials or by satellites. The radio signals allow researchers to map an animal's movements without going anywhere near it.

Radio collars ▲
A lightweight radio collar doesn't stop this harvest mouse clambering up grass stems and behaving normally.

ANIMAL UNDERPASSES

Millions of animals world-wide are killed each year crossing roads. They may be following a regular path in order to feed, or, like toads and some other animals, making an annual migration in order to breed. In some places, special tunnels have been built to help animals avoid roads.

◄ **Toad tunnel**
A toad emerges from an under-road tunnel in Sussex, England. Toads cross roads when returning to their home ponds in spring to breed. Tunnels like this one greatly reduce the numbers of toads killed by traffic.

WHERE TO LOOK

Wherever you go, be on the lookout for trails and traces.
• Gardens
• Woodlands and forest
• Edges of fields
• Open heath and moorland
• Dry scrub
• Coastal areas

ANIMAL TRACES

Whenever you go out nature ranging, keep an eye out for anything that may have been left behind by a passing animal. Even a tiny scrap of fur left on a fence or bush can help you to identify a recent visitor. Other things to look out for are feathers from a moulting bird or even a discarded snake skin. These vital clues can help you put together a picture of the animals that live in your area, even though you may rarely spot the animals themselves.

Snake skin ►
This grass snake has just shed its scaly skin. Snakes do this when their skin gets too small for their growing body. Look out for snake skins and see if you can identify their owners.

Fur deposit ►
When they are on the move, mammals rub against sharp objects, such as thorns, leaving behind tufts of fur that can identify them. Here, a rabbit has left some of its fur on a barbed wire fence.

Snail trail ►
A shiny, silvery trail is a sure sign that a snail or slug has recently passed that way. They produce a film of slippery mucus that helps them to glide over paths, walls, or leaves.

Missing bark ►
Some mammals use trees as "itching posts". This red deer is using a branch to rub the "felt" off its growing antlers. Such rubbing leaves tell-tale marks, but also damages the bark.

Animal footprints

Wild mammals tend to stay out of sight, and some come out only at night. But, even if you don't see an animal, you can detect its presence by the tell-tale footprints it leaves. By identifying tracks you can discover which animals live in your neighbourhood or the places you go nature ranging. Tracks also tell you how animals move. You can produce a permanent record of mammal and other animal tracks by making casts of them using plaster of Paris.

WHAT YOU WILL NEED
- Strip of thin cardboard 25 cm (10 in) long and 4 cm (1.5 in) wide
- Paper clips
- Jug of water
- Mixing bowl or bucket
- Plaster of Paris
- Spoon
- Water
- Old toothbrush

1 Find some animal tracks. Good places to look are shady woodlands or near ponds where there is moist, firm mud or sand. When you find some tracks, look for the clearest ones. Shown above are clear examples of deer footprints.

2 Remove any loose twigs or leaves from the footprints. Shape the strip of cardboard into a ring, securing it with the paper clips. Push the ring downwards so it surrounds the footprints. Make sure there are no gaps around the bottom.

3 Put some plaster of Paris into the bowl. Slowly pour water from the jug into the bowl, stirring the mixture continually with the spoon. When you have smooth, slightly runny plaster, pour it into the cardboard ring.

OBSERVING TRACKS

When you come across tracks, count the number of toes, and look out for claw marks. Also look at the shape of the footprints. Some mammals, including dogs and cats, walk on their toes, while others walk with their heels flat on the ground.

Front

Hind

Dog family ▲
Members of the dog family, such as foxes and wolves, show four toes in both front and hind feet. They also leave claw marks.

Front

Hind

Cat family ▲
Cat footprints, such as lynx and bobcat, show four front and hind toes. There are no claw marks – claws are pulled in when walking.

FOOTPRINTS IN THE SNOW

A snowy winter's day can provide a good opportunity to search for animal tracks. Snow is a great surface for spotting footprints – in this case, those of a snowshoe hare. Hares and rabbits move by hopping or bounding. They push off with their long, powerful hind feet and land on their smaller front feet. Their hind feet land just ahead of their front feet ready to push off again.

Snowshoe hare tracks

Deer

These animals belong to the group of even-toed, hoofed mammals that also includes pigs and cattle. The twin, hoofed toes on each foot leave an easily recognized, footprint.

4 **Leave the plaster** to set for about 15 minutes. Then, lift up the plaster – complete with the cardboard ring – take it home, and leave for a further 24 hours to set completely. Brush off any remaining mud with the old toothbrush. Try to identify which animal made the print.

Front **Hind**

Mustelid family ▲
Animals of the mustelid family, such as otters and badgers, have five front and hind toes. They also have extended claws.

Front **Hind**

Rodents ▲
Squirrels and other rodents walk flat on their feet. They have four front and five hind toes. They also have claws.

Front **Hind**

Rabbits and hares ▶
With four toes, front and rear, rabbit and hare tracks are easy to identify because the hind foot is much longer than the front.

Bones and teeth

When animals die, their skin, muscles, and other soft parts soon rot away or are eaten by other animals. But their bones and teeth remain – and can tell you a lot about the animal they once belonged to. When you go nature ranging, look out for skulls and other bones and see if you can tell what animal they came from. Some biologists clean the bones from dead animals and rebuild their skeletons for further study.

IMPORTANT
When handling bones always wear rubber gloves and wash the gloves afterwards.

Necrophagous beetles
The word necrophagous means "eating the dead" and that's exactly what these beetles do. Here you can see one feeding on a dead shrew. Some biologists use these beetles to strip soft tissues from animals that died naturally in the wild, so that only the skeleton is left.

BONE STRUCTURE

If you find long bones, such as leg bones, you may be able to tell whether they come from mammals or birds. Bird bones are lighter for their size because they are either hollow or contain air spaces reinforced by a honeycomb of struts. A bird's light skeleton makes flight possible.

Mammal and bird bones ▶
As you can see, the structure of a mammal bone is thicker and heavier than that of a bird bone. A bird bone only has a thin outer layer surrounding a large space.

Bird bone

Cow bone

DENTAL CHECK
In open country or woodland you may find a mammal skull, such as the ones shown here. The shape and teeth can identify its owner and its diet. There are four types of mammal teeth. Incisors at the front bite and slice. Canines pierce and grip. Large premolars and molars at the back grind or cut.

Chisel-like incisor teeth

Hedgehog ▲
The hedgehog's big incisors, and sharp, biting premolars and molars, are ideal for its varied diet, which includes beetles, worms, and slugs, as well as birds' eggs and carrion.

Rabbit ▲
Hares and rabbits are herbivores with long, gnawing incisors. These teeth grow constantly so they don't wear down as they slide past each other to slice off pieces of grass.

SKELETONS

You may have seen skeletons like this squirrel skeleton. It shows the features of most rodents – short limbs, gnawing incisor teeth, and long hind feet. These skeletons are produced in various ways. The soft tissues of the dead animal can be removed by burying it so they decay or by exposing it to necrophagous beetles. The separate bones are cleaned and sterilized, then dried and assembled into a skeleton.

Skeleton of a squirrel

Fox ▼
Meat-eaters, such as this fox, use their long canines for grabbing and holding prey, sharp incisors to cut meat, and the sharp edges of their molar teeth to slice through flesh and crack bones.

Pointed canine tooth

Grinding premolar teeth

Deer ▲
Herbivores such as deer and goats eat a diet of plants. Incisors in the lower jaw press against a hard pad in the upper jaw to grab vegetation. Large, flattened premolars and molars move side-to-side, grinding tough plants into pulp.

Food clues

When some animals feed they leave behind no traces of what they ate. Many animals, however, are much messier, and leave clues that show what they are and what they've been eating. Look carefully when you're exploring nature and you'll soon notice plenty of these clues, enabling you to build up a list of the animals that live in an area. For example, if you find an animal corpse, a quick look may reveal what kind of animal made the kill. If you find chewed leaves or nuts, you may even be able to tell which animal did the chewing.

Wings are tough and rarely eaten

Just wings

Bird wings can indicate a kill by a fox or coyote, or by a bird of prey. Wings are often left behind because they contain little meat. These wings mark the spot where a fox killed a jay. A bird of prey usually leaves a ring of neatly plucked feathers.

Chipmunk gnaws a nut held in its front paws

Gnawed nuts

Rodents use their chisel-like teeth to gnaw into hard nuts to reach the seed inside. The remains of the shell can identify which rodent was feeding. Chipmunks and squirrels, for example, split nuts cleanly in half.

Caterpillar of common mormon butterfly

Chewed leaves

Lots of insects eat leaves. Many favour specific plants, or feed in a particular way. Beetles, for example, often cut pieces from the middle of leaves, while caterpillars bite bits from the edge.

Caterpillars chew leaf margins

Fish heads

You may find fish heads, tails, or other chewed remains on the banks of clean freshwater streams or ponds, or on some isolated seashores. This can indicate the presence of otters.

Smashed whelk shells

Crushed winkle shells

Broken crab claws

Open mussel shells

Gull garbage

On rocky shores many animals are encased in a shell or hard case. Hungry gulls get around this by dropping their prey onto rocks to smash the outer covering so the juicy flesh can be extracted.

FOOD STORES

Some animals cache, or store, food for future use. In summer and autumn, for example, you may see squirrels or jays burying seeds and nuts that they will retrieve in winter when food is in short supply. Orb web spiders wrap up prey in silk packages for eating later. If you come across a small animal impaled on a thorn or the spike of a barbed wire fence, you may have found a shrike's larder.

Shrike's larder ▲
Great grey shrikes feed on small mammals, reptiles, amphibians, and insects. Here, one has impaled a sparrow on a tree thorn, which will act as a "larder" until the bird is ready to eat its prey.

Animal droppings

All animals leave behind droppings, or scats, as they're sometimes known. For nature rangers, droppings are a mine of information, and it's quite safe to study them as long as you don't touch them with bare hands. A professional naturalist can tell which animal produced droppings and when, what the animal had eaten, how big it was, and what sex. Don't expect to be able to do this when you start, but you will soon be able to tell the difference between different types of mammal droppings.

WHAT TO LOOK FOR

- Tube-shaped droppings, perhaps with pointed end (fox, raccoon, skunk, opossum, or bear)
- Thinner, rounded tube (cats, such as lynx)
- Long, thin (weasel or stoat)
- Rounded with plant fibre content (deer, rabbits, or hares)
- Rice-grain shaped (rats and other rodents)

CLEAN-UP SQUAD

What happens to animal droppings? Most are broken down by soil fungi and bacteria. But some are dealt with by a clean-up squad of insects. For example, you might spot a dung beetle pushing a ball of dung away to an underground nest. In the nest, a female beetle lays her eggs in the dung. When her young hatch, they emerge into an instant food supply.

Dung beetle rolling a ball of dung

DROPPINGS GALLERY

By examining droppings you can get a good idea of which animal passed by recently, and what it ate. Herbivore droppings are rounded with traces of indigestible plant fibres. Carnivore droppings are usually long and may contain fur, bones, and other prey remains. Here are some common examples of droppings to look out for.

Rabbit droppings ▲
These spherical droppings are very common and are often found in small clumps. Rabbit droppings are dark brown when fresh, but turn greener and paler as they age and dry out.

Deer droppings ▲
The droppings left by deer are dark and cylindrical. Deer eat low-nutrient vegetation so they have to eat a lot to derive any benefit. Hence, they leave behind large amounts of droppings.

Animal latrine

Some mammals leave their droppings in specific locations called latrines. These smelly piles mark out the boundary of that particular animal's territory (in this case a badger's) and warn other members of the same species to stay away.

BIRD PELLETS

At first glance, bird pellets might look like droppings but they are not. So what exactly are they? Birds don't have teeth, so they can't chew their food. Some birds swallow food whole, then regurgitate the hard, indigestible parts of their meal as a soft package called a pellet. Perhaps the most interesting pellets are produced by owls. You can look for these at the bottom of trees or fence posts, or in old barns, where owls roost. Owl pellets can be moistened and gently pulled apart to reveal tiny skulls, bones, and fur.

Owl pellet

Bones found in pellet

Buried droppings

Have you noticed how domestic cats dig a shallow hole to defecate into, then carefully cover their droppings with soil? The same is true for wild species of small cats, such as this bobcat. Sometimes, droppings may also be left in a latrine to mark territory.

IMPORTANT

Never handle animal droppings or pellets with your bare hands. Always wear rubber gloves, which should be washed afterwards.

Otter droppings ▲
Spraints, or otter droppings, are often found on riverbanks. They are irregular in shape, black and sticky when fresh, and contain fish and insect parts. They may be used to mark territory.

Fox droppings ▲
Foxes are omnivores (they eat both plants and meat). So their tubular, sometimes twisted, droppings may contain the fur of small animals, insect wings and casings, or wild fruit seeds.

Wild cat droppings ▲
Cats feed only on other animals. Their droppings can have rounded or tapering ends, and may be divided into smaller pieces. Droppings may contain animal fur.

Hiding and warning

Lots of animals use colours and patterns as a form of disguise – called camouflage – that helps them to blend in with their surroundings. They hide in this way to avoid being eaten by predators or being spotted by their prey. Some poisonous animals use a different strategy – their bright colours and bold patterns act as a warning to predators not to touch them. Recruit some friends to see how camouflage works.

WHAT YOU WILL NEED

- 40 toothpicks
- 2 glasses of water coloured with food dye (1 red and 1 green)
- Kitchen roll
- Stopwatch or watch with a second hand
- Tray
- Two friends

Red toothpicks are easily "caught" because they stand out

ANIMAL MIMICS

Many poisonous animals use bright colours and patterns to warn would-be predators to back off. Some harmless animals mimic these warning colours to fool enemies into thinking they are dangerous, too. For example, the red, black, and yellow bands of the harmless milk snake deter its predators because they mimic those of the highly venomous and deadly coral snake.

The striped pattern is also an excellent camouflage on the forest floor

Brazilian coral snake

Milk snake

(1) **Overnight, soak 20** toothpicks in the green-coloured water and 20 in the red-coloured water. Remove and dry them on the kitchen roll. The toothpicks represent two varieties of the "insect" *Toothpickus vulgaris.*

Staying out of sight

Always look carefully at your surroundings. You never know what may be concealed by camouflage. Take this young fawn, for example, its spotted fur breaks up its outline as it rests in the dappled sunlight.

SCARY INSECTS

On summer walks, take a look at the wings of passing butterflies. Many, such as this South American owl butterfly, have eye-shaped patterns on their wings, which resemble larger animals' eyes. The sudden flash of the eyespots when the wings open or close can startle predators such as small birds. This gives the butterfly vital seconds in which to escape from its enemy.

Eyespot gives impression of an owl's eye

Owl butterfly

IMPORTANT

Make sure that you pick up all the toothpicks from the ground after this activity. Don't leave any in the grass.

④ Put the toothpicks on the tray and count how many red ones and how many green ones your "birds" have caught. You should find they have many more red than green – the green "insects" are much better camouflaged in the green grass.

② Check that it's not going to rain, then – on your own – find a patch of ground where the grass is neither too long nor too short. "Plant" the toothpicks at random in the ground, so that they do not stick up above the tops of the grass.

③ Ask your friends to become birds that prey on *Toothpickus* insects. They can use one hand only – as a bird would use its beak. Give them 30 seconds to get as many toothpicks as they can.

The "birds" find far more red "insects"

Animal homes

Many animals build homes that they occupy for part or all of the year. They use these homes to protect themselves from predators, rain, high winds, and floods, and to provide a safe haven in which to raise their young. Sometimes animals also use their homes to catch and store food. Animal homes include tunnels – especially in open ground such as heathlands and coastal areas – and various types of nests. Homes can be made from mud, sticks, grass, or other locally found materials, or from materials made by the animal itself, such as a spider's silk. A key part of nature ranging is identifying these homes and their occupants. Here are a few examples to help you get started.

Squirrel's drey
On woodland walks look out for a squirrel's drey – shown here opened up – high up in trees. Made from sticks and twigs, and lined with leaves and grasses, this provides a cosy shelter from cold weather.

IMPORTANT

If you find an animal home, do not disturb it, and never put your hand into a nest or burrow in case it contains a dangerous animal.

MOBILE HOMES

At risk of being attacked by predators when looking for food? Why not carry your home around with you, ready to retreat into should danger threaten. Well, that's precisely what some small animals do. For example, molluscs such as snails, periwinkles, and whelks, secrete a spiral shell that protects them and makes them very hard to swallow. A discarded mollusc shell also provides a useful mobile home for the hermit crab.

Hermit crab ▲
This hermit crab is housed in an empty whelk shell. At the first sign of attack, it retreats inside the shell. As the crab grows, it finds a bigger shell to move into.

◄ Underground home

Burrows hide their owners from hungry predators, protect them from bad weather, and may serve as a nesting site. This Atlantic puffin uses a cliff top burrow as a safe place to lay eggs and to raise its young.

▲ Mud house

In midsummer, you may be able to spot the cup-shaped nests of swallows under the eaves of houses or on the rafters of barns. These insect-eating birds build their nests from grass and mud.

Insect trap ►

This web spun by an orb-weaver spider is both a home and a trap for flying insects. Once entangled, the struggling insect makes the web vibrate, alerting the spider, which subdues, then feeds on its prey.

Beaver's lodge ▼

The lodge, or nest, of a family of beavers is made from sticks and mud, and has an underwater entrance. Beavers are big, tree-eating rodents, that live in forest lakes or ponds, formed when they dam streams with branches.

Wildlife at night

Unlike us, many animals hide and rest during the day, only becoming active as it starts to get dark. This nocturnal lifestyle gives animals some invisibility to avoid predators or to ambush prey. It also means that they avoid competition for food and other resources with animals that are active during the day. If you know how to do it, the hours of darkness are a great time to go on an expedition to spot nocturnal wildlife including bats, badgers, and moths.

MOTH TRAP

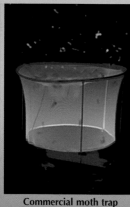

Commercial moth trap

Most moths are active after dark, seeking out night-scented flowers to feed on. You've probably noticed that moths are attracted to light, although no one is exactly sure why. Scientists who study moths take advantage of their attraction to light by setting up moth traps, such as the one shown here. They can then check the number and variety of moths in a particular area.

WHAT YOU WILL NEED

- Torch
- Notebook
- Pen or pencil
- Warm clothes

 Don't go out after dark without an adult.

EYE SHINE

Many nocturnal mammals have a layer called the tapetum inside their eyes that reflects light. This greatly increases sensitivity in dim light or darkness so that animals can see more. The tapetum also reflects torchlight, producing green or red eye shine. Here are some examples.

Racoon

Badger

BAT TRICK

Sensitive ears ▲
Bats pinpoint prey by
sending out pulses of high-
pitched sounds, then listening
for echoes produced when they
bounce off prey.

Long-eared bats

In summer or early autumn, you may notice bats – the only
mammals that can fly – flitting around trees. Bats are
nocturnal and most feed on flying insects, such as moths,
which they catch using a type of "animal sonar" called
echolocation. Try throwing small pellets of bread into the air.
This may trick bats into swooping down to catch their "prey",
and you will see them silhouetted against the twilight sky.

HANDY TIP
Take sandwiches and
a hot drink with you when
you go nature ranging
at night.

Out at night
The key to successful night-time nature ranging is to move quietly
and to wait patiently. Use your torch to find your way around, but
do not leave it on all the time. If you go out on a moonlit night this
will provide you with dim, natural light to see nocturnal animals.

Wild cat

Deer

Wolves

Making a bat box

One in four of all the world's mammals is a bat, so no matter where you are, it is likely there are bats living nearby. Here we show you how to build a safe, comfortable box where bats can live and breed. It may take a few months for bats to start using this new home, so be patient. Look out for droppings, urine staining, and "chattering", which are all signs that the box is occupied.

HANDY TIP

Bats like a clear path to their roost so place the box away from branches and foliage.

WHAT YOU WILL NEED

- Plank of softwood 15 x 113 x 1.5 cm (6 x 45 x ½ in)
- Tape measure
- Ruler
- Pencil
- Saw
- Sandpaper
- Waterproof glue
- Approximately twenty 2.5-cm (1-in) nails
- Hammer
- Two 5-cm (2-in) nails

Adult supervision is needed when using the saw and hammer.

IMPORTANT

Do not use any paint or wood preservatives as bats are sensitive to smells and some chemicals are harmful to bats.

2.5 cm (1 in)

a

b — 20 cm (8 in)

c — 14.5 cm (5¾ in)

d — 9 cm (3½ in)

e — 33 cm (13 in)

113 cm (45 in)

f — 14 cm (5½ in) / 20 cm (8 in)

g — 20 cm (8 in) / 14 cm (5½ in)

15 cm (6 in)

1 Use the tape measure, ruler, and pencil to mark up the plank of wood and then letter each piece as shown. Saw along the lines and sand away any rough edges.

2 On the back plate (e), draw a pencil line 4 cm (1½ in) from the top. Glue down the edge of the strip of wood (a) along that line. Secure from the back with nails.

3 Rough up the interior walls using the teeth of the saw. This is so the bat can get a better grip. Glue the edges of side panels (f and g) onto the back plate (e), so that the top edges are glued 2.5 cm (1 in) beneath the strip (a). Secure with nails.

Seeing bats

Bat droppings under your bat box are a sure sign it is occupied. The best time to see "your" bats in flight is around dusk. To increase the chance of bats taking up residence, make sure your bat box is sheltered from strong winds, exposed to sun for part of the day, and placed high up the tree to be safe from cats

Ask an adult to help you nail the box to a tree trunk

4 **Glue the** front panel (c) onto the front edges of side pieces (f and g), making sure that the panel juts out at the bottom by 1.5 cm ($\frac{1}{2}$ in). Adjust if the plank of wood is slightly thicker. Secure with nails.

5 **Glue and nail** the base (d), leaving a 6 cm (2 $\frac{1}{2}$ in) slit at the back. Place two nails on the roof (b) 3 cm (1 in) from each edge and about 4 cm (1 $\frac{1}{4}$ in) from the front to act as a stop inside the box. Nail the top and bottom of the box to a tree, using two 5-cm (2-in) nails.

BATS IN THE WILD

In the wild, bats roost (rest and sleep) in places that provide shelter from predators or from bad weather. These roosting places include caves, abandoned buildings, old mines, underneath bridges, or, in warmer parts of the world, in tree branches. Most bats roost together in colonies that can contain thousands or even millions of bats.

Roosting fruit bats ▶
Hanging upside-down with wings folded, a colony of fruit bats roost in a cave in Thailand.

Plant planet

The Earth's land surface provides a home for an astonishing variety of plants. They have the unique ability to make their own food by photosynthesis. This is the process by which plants use the green chlorophyll that colours their leaves to trap the Sun's energy to make sugars. Photosynthesis also releases the oxygen that you and other organisms breathe in. You can use pondweed to see the process in action.

Test tube is full of water at the beginning of the experiment

In sunlight, the pondweed slowly releases tiny oxygen bubbles

Pondweed in upside-down funnel

1 **Half fill** a sink with cold water. Hold the jar underwater, put some pondweed in it, then place the funnel upside-down inside the jar to "trap" the pondweed.

WHAT YOU WILL NEED

- Glass jar
- Test tube
- Wide-necked funnel
- Pondweed, such as hornwort or elodea
- Wooden splint or taper
- Matches
- Water

An adult should help you when you use the matches and splint.

2 **Now hold** the test tube underwater so it fills with water. After making sure there is no air inside the test tube, carefully slide its open end over the spout of the funnel.

3 **Keeping the jar**, funnel, and test tube upright, remove them together from the water in the sink. Carefully tip a little water from the jar so it does not spill over. Place the assembled equipment indoors on a sunny windowsill.

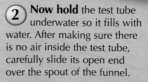

After a few hours in sunlight, the test tube fills with oxygen

PLANT CENSUS

Wherever you look, there are often many different plants living side by side. You can find out how many by carrying out a plant census. You need a measuring square called a quadrat. Throw the quadrat at random over an area of ground, then record the plants in each small square to make a quadrat map.

Quadrat ▲
A quadrat consists of a square wooden frame divided into 16 smaller squares by six pieces of string or wire.

④ When the tube is nearly filled with oxygen, put your thumb over the end of the tube and remove it from the jar.

⑤ Ask an adult to light the splint, blow it out, then put the glowing tip into the test tube. It will relight, showing that pure oxygen is present.

THE WORLD OF PLANTS

There are 300,000 different plant types on Earth, but most belong to one of four groups that you will easily recognize.

Flowering plants ▼
Around 80 per cent of all plants reproduce using flowers that produce seeds. The biggest are broad-leaved trees, such as oaks. The smallest is tiny duckweed, which floats on ponds.

Dog rose

◄ Conifers
Pines, firs, spruces, cedars, and other conifers produce seeds in cones instead of flowers.

Scots pine

Ferns ►
Fond of damp, shady places, ferns have fronds, or leaves, divided into leaflets. They reproduce by releasing spores.

Buckler fern

Mosses and liverworts ▼
These small, delicate plants grow in clumps in damp and wet places. They have no true roots or leaves, and reproduce using spores.

Moss

Secret senses

Plants may not have eyes, but they can tell where the Sun is. Their stems move as they grow towards the Sun, searching out the light needed for photosynthesis. They can also tell "up" from "down" by sensing gravity. You can watch this happen by putting a plant inside a box and seeing how light steers its growth.

Tracking the Sun
Many plants follow the Sun, turning their leaves towards it as the Sun moves across the sky. Sunflowers, as their name implies, have flowers that track the Sun. Try watching them on a sunny day.

> **HANDY TIP**
> Fit the lid of the shoebox carefully to stop any stray light getting in.

Cardboard flaps are held in place by tape

1 **Cut out two** identical pieces of cardboard, as deep as the shoebox and two-thirds as wide. Tape them in the box as shown. Then cut a small hole in one end of the box.

2 **Paint the inside** of the box matt black to reduce light reflection – include the flaps and the lid.

3 **Turn the box** upright with the hole at the top. Put some compost in the flowerpot, plant a bean seed about 2 cm (¾ in) below the surface, and water the pot. Put the pot in the box and fit the lid.

WHAT YOU WILL NEED

- Shoebox with lid
- Cardboard
- Scissors
- Matt black paint
- Paintbrush
- Tape
- Flowerpot
- Potting compost
- Runner bean seed
- Notebook and/or digital camera

INSECT TRAPPERS

"Teeth"

Sensitive hair

Some plants can move amazingly fast. This Venus flytrap is a bog plant that lives in poor soil. It "eats" insects for extra nutrients. If an insect touches the plant's sensitive hairs, the hinged leaves snap shut. The insect is trapped and digested.

◄ **Doomed damsel**
This damselfly is about to trigger the trap. "Teeth" at the edge of each pad act as prison bars to prevent escape.

*Emerging shoot grows
upwards towards the light*

4 **Remove the lid** at the same time
each day to check what is happening.
Record your findings using your notebook
or digital camera. Note how the bean plant
grows, and how readily it finds its way
towards light. Add a little water each day
to keep the compost moist.

*Plant grows
around the
cardboard flap
as it seeks out
light entering
through the
hole above*

*Bean plant
emerges from
the germinating
seed within
the compost*

GETTING A GRIP

Another way for plants to reach
light is to grip other plants. This
passionflower – just like vines,
peas, and cucumber – uses spring-
like tendrils to pull itself up. The
tendril tip winds around something
solid, and the rest of the tendril
coils up to pull the plant upwards.
Stroke the end of a tendril with a
matchstick and watch it curl.

Passionflower

WHAT YOU WILL NEED

- Two drinking glasses
- Food dye
- Water
- Spoon
- Pale-coloured flower with a long stem, such as a white carnation
- Sticky tape
- Sharp knife

Ask an adult to split the stem.

Thirsty work

Plants need lots of water to grow and stay alive. Water also keeps plant cells firm, holding plants upright and in shape. Without water, plants wilt and die. Plants take in water through their roots. It travels up microscopic pipelines in their stems to leaves and flowers. From here, much of the water evaporates into the air as water vapour. This process, called transpiration, provides the "pull" that draws up more water through roots and stems. You can see water moving up a plant in this simple experiment.

1 **Lay the flower** carefully on a cutting surface. Ask an adult to slice its stem in two, working from the base of the stem to around halfway up.

2 **Wind some** tape around the stem just above the top end of the cut. This prevents the stem from splitting any further. Each half stem contains water-transporting tubes.

Sticky tape prevents upper part of stem from splitting

3 **Pour water into** both glasses until they are three-quarters full. Add food dye to one glass and stir well.

STORING WATER

While most plants need a constant supply of water, some plants have an amazing ability to store water for long periods of time. The most obvious are desert plants such as cacti, which store water from infrequent rain in their thick, expandable stems. Some rainforest plants also store water. These stores can sometimes provide a life-saving drink of clean water for people able to identify the right plants.

Water vine ▶
A forest dweller drinks water from a water vine in the Amazonian rainforest in Brazil. He has cut into the vine to release the fresh, clean water.

Dye left behind in petals as water evaporates into the air

These petals stay white because they receive plain water from the left-hand glass

Separate mini-tubes in stem carry plain water and coloured water

MAKING WEATHER

Around the equator, where temperatures are high all year, tropical rainforests create their own weather. When daily rain soaks the forest soil, millions of trees, shrubs, and plants take up the water. This water evaporates from their leaves as water vapour, which forms clouds above the rainforest. Eventually, more rain falls from these clouds.

Tropical rainforest ▲
This aerial view of a lowland rainforest in the Danum Valley in Borneo shows rain clouds forming above the treetops following heavy rain.

Tiny tubes carry water and dye up this half of the stem

Red food dye is dissolved in this glass of water

Glass contains plain water without any dye

4 **Put each half-stem** into one of the glasses. Support the flower by leaning it against a wall or window. Leave the flower to take up water. Come back every 15 minutes to look at the petals.

5 **Within one hour** you should see half of the flower changing colour. This indicates that water is travelling up the stem and into the flower. This is happening along both half stems but is only visible on the coloured side where the water reaching the flower contains the dye.

Studying flowers

We all enjoy the colours and scents of flowers. More importantly, because flowers make and release seeds, they play a vital part in a plant's life cycle. It's fascinating to look at the many different types of flowers. Most last only a short time before they wither. However, if you press them, the dried flowers can last for years.

Flowers arranged on blotting paper

1 Collect some plants with their flowers. If possible, identify the flowers using a plant guide or by asking an adult who can recognize them. Pressing works best for freshly picked flowers. By squeezing out moisture, it dries the flower and stops it from rotting.

2 Put a sheet of blotting paper on a book or board. Arrange the flowers on the blotting paper, but not too close together. Cover them with another sheet of blotting paper.

WHAT YOU WILL NEED

- Some heavy books and/or wooden boards
- Blotting paper
- Flowers
- Plant guide
- Tape or PVA glue

IMPORTANT

Many wild flowers are protected by law, so it is illegal to pick them. If you want to press flowers, ask an adult which ones you can use.

PARTS OF A FLOWER

All flowers share the same basic parts. Petals protect the flower and attract pollinating animals. Stalked anthers produce pollen, which contain male cells. These fertilize female cells inside the central ovary to produce seeds.

Anther

Petal

Ovary

Inside view ▶
Cut in half, this dwarf Iceland poppy flower reveals its parts. Ask an adult to cut a flower in half so you can see what's inside.

OPENING AND CLOSING

Watch out for flowers opening and closing. Flowers are easily damaged by cold or heavy rain. So many plants protect their flowers by closing them at night, when temperatures drop, or if the sky darkens with clouds during the day.

Morning glory ▶
These flowers open in sunshine but close at dusk or if it is cloudy. They also change colour according to the temperature.

FLOWERHEADS

On some plants, flowers grow singly on long stems. On others, flowers develop in clusters called flowerheads or inflorescences. These include spikes, umbels, and composite flowers.

Single flower ▶
This hibiscus has separate, single flowers that grow on their own stalk, as do dog roses and lilies. Some plants, such as tulips, have only one flower.

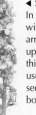

◀ Spike
In a spike, flowers without stalks are arranged on a single upright stem, as in this mullein. Flowers usually open in sequence, from the bottom upwards.

③ **Place a heavy** weight – such as a pile of books – on top of the piece of blotting paper. Leave in position for about two weeks. This will give time for the paper to absorb water from the flowers so that they dry out.

Heavy books press flowers below

Umbel ▶
This hogweed shows an umbel arrangement. Small flowers arise from the same level on the stem to form an umbrella-like flowerhead that also provides insects with somewhere to land.

▼ Composite flower
At the centre of this sunflower are tight clusters of tiny flowers, called florets. These form a flowerhead that resembles a single flower.

④ **After two weeks**, carefully remove the weight and top sheet of blotting paper. Now arrange, and name, the dried flowers in your nature diary, but remember that they are quite fragile. Fix the pressed flowers in place using thin strips of tape or PVA glue.

Pollination

Flowers don't grow just for us to admire. They make pollen, which is carried to other flowers of the same kind. This is called pollination. The pollen is used to make seeds. Some flowers use wind to spread pollen, but many depend on animal visitors, such as insects, to pollinate their flowers. Attracted by a flower's bright colours and strong smells, animals come to feed on nectar, a sweet-tasting liquid food. While they are there, animals pick up pollen and carry it to other flowers. When animals pollinate flowers they are often too busy to worry about being watched, so you may be able to observe them quite closely.

Long tongues
Look out for butterflies visiting sweet-smelling flowers, such as buddleia or this marjoram. They uncoil their tongue to reach the nectar at the bottom of narrow, tube-shaped flowers.

IMPORTANT

Don't touch or get too close to bees while they are visiting flowers because they may sting you.

ALL ABOUT POLLEN

Pollen consists of tiny specks called pollen grains made by anthers, the male parts of the flower. In wind-pollinated flowers the grains are light and dusty, but in animal-pollinated flowers they are often sticky. During pollination, pollen grains are carried to the female part of the same kind of flower, where seeds are made.

◄ **Anthers and stigma**
Anthers (blue and white) surround the stigma (red), the tip of the flower's female part, which receives pollen.

Blowing in the wind

On dry, summer days look out for grasses shedding clouds of pollen. Grasses and other wind-pollinated plants release thousands of pollen grains into the wind. Their flowers are small, drab, and smell-free because, being wind-pollinated, they don't need to attract insects.

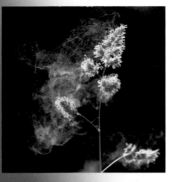

POLLINATING BIRDS

In some parts of the world – the Americas, Africa, Asia, and Australia – birds as well as insects pollinate flowers. Some, such as honey creepers, clamber over flowers as they search for nectar, accidentally picking up pollen at the same time. But hummingbirds feed while hovering in mid-air. Spotting bird-pollinated flowers is easy. Most of them are yellow or red, and they rarely smell.

Hummingbird ▶
A summer visitor to eastern North America, this ruby-throated hummingbird hovers as it feeds on the flower's nectar.

WHERE TO LOOK

- Look for bees on bright, showy flowers, especially blue, purple, or yellow ones.
- Look for butterflies on buddleia or other tube-shaped, scented flowers.
- Look for birds on red and yellow flowers, such as poinsettia.

Honey guides

Pollinating insects, such as this bumblebee targeting a foxglove, are helped in their search for nectar. They are often directed towards a flower's nectar stores by dots or lines on its petals called honey guides.

Honey guides

Spreading seeds

Plants need to disperse, or spread, their seeds far and wide so they have enough space, water, and light to sprout and grow. Seeds develop inside fruits that help them to disperse by various routes – wind, animals, water, and even by explosive force. In the summer, look for tricks used by plants to spread seeds. Some seeds spread by sticking to fur or feathers – or to your socks and shoes. After a nature-ranging walk, find out whether you have given any seeds a lift home.

WHAT YOU WILL NEED

- Metal baking tray
- Compost
- Blunt knife or screwdriver
- Water sprayer or indoor watering can
- Clingfilm or polythene bag

Ask an adult to supervise putting the tray into, and removing it from, the oven.

1 **Put a layer** of compost in the baking tray. Preheat the oven to 100°C (210°F). Place the tray in the oven and "bake" the compost for 30 minutes. This will kill any seeds that are already in the compost.

3 **Use the knife** or screwdriver to scrape the soles of your walking shoes onto the compost. Water the compost, seal it with the bag or clingfilm, and put it on a sunny windowsill.

Grass grows from the picked-up seeds

2 **Using oven gloves,** remove the baking tray from the oven. Leave it to cool in a safe location.

HANDY TIP

Wear trainers or walking boots so that seeds get trapped in the treads.

TASTY FRUITS

Some plants produce sweet, juicy fruits that attract and provide food for many birds and mammals, including ourselves. Once eaten, the fruit is digested but the seeds pass unharmed out of the animal's body in its droppings. Animals are always on the move and so the seeds are deposited well away from their parent plant – and in a "starter kit" of natural fertilizer.

◄ **Berry eater**
A young northern mockingbird eats the juicy, purple berries of the pokeweed plant. The seeds in the bird's droppings will be deposited elsewhere, allowing new pokeweed plants to thrive.

④ During the next 10 days, check the tray regularly and keep the compost moist. You should soon see new plants sprouting from the seeds picked up by your shoes.

Newly sprouted plant grows towards the light

SNAPPING, DRIFTING, AND FLOATING

Not all seeds are spread by animals. Some are flung explosively into the air, blown by wind, or dispersed by oceans and rivers.

Snapping pods ►
On warm summer days, listen for sharp snapping sounds coming from overgrown places and shrubs. These sounds are made by pods (fruits) that snap open as they dry out, flinging their seeds through the air.

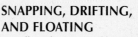

Exploding pod throws out the seeds

Cow vetch

Drifting away ▲
Many plants produce fruits with wings, fluffy sails, or – like this dandelion – individual parachutes. In dry weather, the seedheads open out, and seeds drift away in the wind.

Floating seeds ►
A few plants depend on water to help them spread their seeds. You might see them washed up on a beach. Their fruits are designed to float, sometimes – as with this sprouting coconut – over long distances.

Starting life

Most plants start life as a seed, a living package consisting of a baby plant and its food store. Seeds only start to grow, or germinate, when conditions – such as moisture and warmth – are just right. Some seeds germinate soon after being released from their parent plant. Others can remain dormant, or "sleeping", for months or years. During germination, a seed soaks up water, splits open, and the young plant's root grows downwards, and its shoot grows upwards. Most seeds germinate underground, so you can't see what happens. But if you "sow" a seed in a glass, you can see it come to life.

WHAT YOU WILL NEED

- Broad bean seed
- Drinking glass
- Sheet of blotting paper
- Cotton wool
- Water
- Notebook and/or digital camera

Seed takes in water and starts to grow

Day 1

DESERT IN BLOOM

It's not just tough plants, such as cacti, that can live in hot, dry deserts. Some smaller plants can survive, too. Their seeds stay dormant in the dry desert soil for months or years until it rains. Then, just briefly, the desert comes into bloom. As rain soaks into the desert soil, the dormant seeds "wake up" and germinate. Within days, plants grow and flower, shed their seeds, then wither and die, not to be seen until it rains again.

Desert before rainfall

Desert after rainfall

1 **Line the inside** of the glass with the blotting paper. Push the cotton wool into the middle of the glass. Put the broad bean seed halfway down the glass between the blotting paper and the glass.

HANDY TIP

In spring and summer look out for growing shoots as seeds germinate in gardens and woodland.

SPREADING WITHOUT SEEDS

This strawberry plant is one of many types of plant that spread not only through seeds but also by sending out side shoots called runners. Runners take root away from their parent to produce small plantlets that grow into new plants. Look for runners when you are nature ranging. Lift up a runner and several plantlets should be attached.

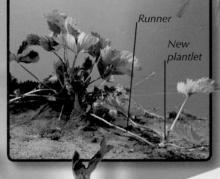

Runner

New plantlet

Leaves use sunlight to make food for the growing plant

Root takes in water and anchors the plant

2 **Add some water** to the glass, but only to a level below the seed. (If you cover the seed with water, it won't germinate or grow.) The water soaks into the cotton wool and rises up through the blotting paper. Leave the glass in a warm, dark place so that the seed can germinate.

Food store inside the seed is used up as the shoot and root grow

3 **Check the glass** each day for the next 14 days, topping up the water daily. Record what you see in your notebook and/or with your camera. As the seed germinates a root appears, followed by a shoot. When leaves appear, leave the glass in the light.

Day 8

Day 14

Treewatch

Trees form a vital part of the living world. They release oxygen into the air and absorb carbon dioxide, and their branches, leaves, and seeds provide shelter and food for many animals. Trees are also the tallest and longest-lived plants in the world. Here, you can find out the height and age of a tree.

WHAT YOU WILL NEED

- Measuring tape
- Long stick or cane
- Pencil and notebook
- Calculator
- A friend to help you

Tip of pencil in line with top of tree

1 **Choose a tree.** Stand facing, and some distance away from, the tree. Ask your friend to stand at the bottom of the tree with the stick.

2 **Hold out** the pencil at arm's length and line it up so that the top of the pencil is level with the top of the tree. Still keeping the pencil in position, move your thumb down the pencil so it is level with the bottom of the tree.

Thumb in line with the bottom of tree

HOW OLD?

Which trees? ▲
This method works for most trees except for fast growers (firs) and slow growers (horse chestnuts).

One way of working out the age of a tree is to count the growth rings that radiate from the centre of its trunk. Unfortunately, you have to cut down the tree first! So here's a simpler way of estimating a tree's age. Take a tape measure and measure the circumference (distance round) of the trunk in centimetres at a point 1.5 m (5 ft) above the ground. Using a calculator, divide the circumference by 2.5 to get the tree's age in years.

BROAD-LEAVED TREES AND CONIFERS

It's easy to tell whether a tree is broad-leaved or a conifer. Broad-leaved trees, such as oaks, birches, and cherries, have broad, thin leaves and flowers that develop seeds. Broad-leaved trees often shed their leaves in autumn. Conifers, such as firs, pines, and spruces, have narrow, hard leaves that are needle- or scale-shaped. Conifers produce their seeds in cones, are evergreen, and they often smell aromatic.

Oak

Scots pine

Try to find out whether the tree is a broad-leaved tree or a conifer, and what species

This distance is the height of the tree

3 **Keeping your thumb** in place, turn the pencil so it is horizontal. Ask your friend to walk away from the trunk. Tell them to stop when level with the tip of the pencil, and to mark the spot with the stick.

4 **Now measure** with the tape the distance from the stick to the base of the tree and record it in your notebook. This is the height of the tree. Try to find out the name of the tree.

Bark

Run your fingers over a tree's trunk and feel the texture of its bark. Just as skin protects your insides from the outside world, so bark surrounds and protects a tree, defending it from attack by fungi and animals, and stopping it from drying out. Bark also contains tiny pores that allow air to reach the tree so it can "breathe". Whether bark is rough or smooth depends on the type of tree and its age. As trees age and expand, their bark develops more cracks and grooves. Here, you can find out how to record bark patterns.

1 **Select a tree** and brush any loose particles from a section of bark. Tape a sheet of paper to that area of the trunk.

2 **Rub the paper** with a wax crayon. This will produce a permanent record of the ridges, furrows, and other patterns in the bark that you can keep in your nature diary.

3 **Carefully remove** the paper from the trunk. If possible, identify the tree using the tree guide, or ask a knowledgeable adult. Make a note of its name – and bark colour – on the paper.

RESISTING POLLUTION

Look out for the London plane tree in city parks and gardens. Its trunk sheds flakes of bark to produce a distinctive pattern of light and dark patches. Shedding removes pollutants that would otherwise block the pores and prevent air from reaching the trunk. It also explains why, in the past, the London plane – but not other trees – thrived in cities with high pollution levels.

◄ **City dweller**
This London plane tree is growing in a square in the middle of London, England.

London plane

Dappled trunk produced by pieces of bark being shed

*Each type of
tree has its
own bark
pattern*

4 **Repeat these steps** with
other types of tree to build up
a portfolio of bark rubbings. While
you are doing this, note any small
animals on the bark or, if you find
a fallen tree, under loose, rotting
bark that can be pulled away.

WHAT YOU WILL NEED

- Wax crayons
- Sheets of thick
  drawing paper
- Tape
- A field guide to trees

Looking at leaves

WHAT YOU WILL NEED

- Fallen leaves
- Saucepan
- 1 l (1³/₄ pts) water
- 40 g (1¹/₂ oz) washing soda crystals
- Rubber gloves
- Blotting paper

Ask an adult to help you when you heat the water and soda.

Without leaves, trees and other plants would not be able to collect the light they need to grow. Evergreen trees keep their leaves all year round, whereas deciduous trees have more delicate leaves that are shed during the coldest times of the year. Leaves are supported by a network of veins that fan out from a central midrib, which arises from the leaf stalk. Veins carry essential materials to and from the leaf's cells. You can make a leaf skeleton by removing the soft parts of the leaf blade to expose the network of veins.

1 **Add the water** to a saucepan along with the washing soda crystals. Heat the pan until the water and washing soda start to boil.

AUTUMN COLOURS

In autumn, the leaves of deciduous trees change colour before they are shed. The chlorophyll that colours leaves green breaks down, and is replaced by other pigments that produce yellows, oranges, and reds.

2 **Remove the pan** from the heat. Put the leaves into the hot washing soda solution and leave there for several hours.

3 **Wearing the** rubber gloves, put the saucepan under a tap and rinse the leaves thoroughly in cold water. Washing removes the soft parts of the leaf, so that a "skeleton" of midrib and veins is left behind. Dry the leaf skeletons on the blotting paper and then stick them into your nature notebook.

LEAF PRINTS

You can make leaf prints in much the same way you make bark rubbings. To record the different shapes and textures of leaves put a leaf on a smooth surface and cover it with a piece of white paper. Holding the paper in place, rub over the leaf with a soft coloured pencil or wax crayon.

◄ **Colourful copies**
Leaf prints record not just a leaf's shape but also its pattern of veins. Try to label each rubbing with the tree that the leaf came from.

Veins are visible on the leaf after washing with soda water

LEAF TYPES

The leaves of broad-leaved trees (dicot flowering plants) have branching veins and include simple and compound types. Palm trees have broad fronds. Conifer leaves are narrow and leathery.

Simple leaf ▶
A simple leaf, such as this maple, consists of a single leaf blade that is not divided. Both simple and compound leaves are classified by shape.

Maple

◄ **Compound leaf**
This leaf may look like many leaves but it is actually a single leaf, called a compound leaf. It is divided into many small leaflets attached to a central stalk.

Mountain ash

Palm leaf ▶
Palms are trees that belong to a group of flowering plants called monocots. Their leaves are frond-like and have parallel veins.

Brazilian wax palm

◄ **Conifer leaf**
Mostly evergreen, conifers have hard needle- or scale-like leaves that can tolerate dry or cold conditions. Conifers produce seeds in cones, not in flowers.

Santa Lucia fir

IMPORTANT
Washing soda can harm the skin — always wear rubber gloves when handling the soaked leaves.

Cones

Wherever pines, firs, or other conifers grow, it's fun to collect the cones that fall from these trees onto the woodland floor. Some cones are tiny, but others are huge, weighing up to five kilos (11 lbs). Just as broad-leaved trees use flowers to make their seeds, conifers use cones to make seeds. Collect some ripe female cones and watch how their scales open with the changing weather.

Deodar cedar cone

Big-cone pine cone

White spruce cone

Single-leaf pinyon cone

1 **Visit a coniferous** woodland (one with trees such as pines, firs, and spruces). Collect some cones in your bag and take them home with you.

Scales are closed on this damp cone

Scales open up in warm, dry weather

SEED EATERS

Conifer seeds are an important food source for forest birds and small mammals. For example, crossbills and nutcrackers have specialized beaks to probe for and extract seeds from cones, while red squirrels get at seeds by stripping off cone scales.

◄ **Crossbill**
This red crossbill's beak has a crossed tip to help it lift the scales of a cone and loosen the seeds.

2 **If possible**, identify the cones and put them in a warm, dry place. If the scales of the cones are closed, watch them over several days to see if the scales open. This normally happens in warm, dry weather, ideal conditions for the cone to release its seeds.

- Bag for collecting cones
- Tweezers

Only go into a woodland when accompanied by an adult.

Woody scales protect seeds inside the cone

MALE AND FEMALE CONES

Conifers reproduce using male and female cones, which usually grow separately on the same tree. Male cones tend to be soft and smaller than female cones. If you tap them, they release clouds of pollen. This pollen is carried by the wind to pollinate the female cones, which then produce seeds. Once this has happened, the female cone's scales close and become increasingly woody as the seeds develop, a process that can take up to three years. When the cone is mature, and the weather is neither too damp nor too cold, the scales open and seeds are released.

Male cone

Mature female cone

Seed

Scots pine cones ▶
The difference between these male and female cones is clear. Once male cones have shed their pollen, they drop off. Years after pollination, the woody female cone releases its seeds, which spin away.

3 **If the scales** are open, look inside to see if there is a seed. Most conifers have seeds with papery "wings". Use the tweezers to remove a seed without tearing the wing. Hold the seed up in the air. Let it go and watch it spiral to the floor. If caught by the wind, this takes the seed well away from its parent plant.

WHAT YOU WILL NEED

- Aquarium tank (made of glass or plastic) with a lid
- Trowel
- Shallow bowl
- Spray bottle filled with water
- 3 plastic bags
- Woodland soil
- Leaf litter
- Pine cones (if present)
- Small dead branches
- Magnifying glass

⚠ Ask an adult to accompany you when you visit a woodland.

Woodlands

Deciduous woodlands have broad-leaved trees, such as oaks, birches, and maples, that lose their leaves in autumn. They provide food and a home for animals such as squirrels and deer, and for many smaller creatures that live in the rotting leaves – the leaf litter – that cover the woodland floor. Find out more about leaf litter dwellers by making a woodland terrarium.

Lid prevents animals from escaping

1 **Visit a woodland** – preferably one where there is a mix of different types of deciduous trees. Use the trowel to collect both dry and moist leaf litter from different locations. Put the litter into one of the plastic bags.

2 **Use the trowel** to dig up several samples of woodland soil from different locations. Put this into the second bag. Collect some dead branches, scraps of bark, and any pine cones, and put these into the third bag.

Bowl half-filled with water

Collect enough woodland soil to cover the bottom of the tank

IMPORTANT

When you have finished with your terrarium, return the leaf litter and its animals back to their woodland.

3 **Back at home** you can now assemble your terrarium. Cover the floor of the aquarium tank with woodland soil. Put the bowl in one corner, fix it in place with more soil, then half fill it with water.

4 **Put the leaf** litter, fir cones, and bark scraps in the tank (don't fill it more than halfway). Angle one or two branches across the leaf litter. Spray a little water over the leaf litter and soil to keep it damp. Put the lid on the tank.

TREE SURVEY

How varied are the woodlands you visit? The number and variety of trees in a woodland depends on its age, whether its soil is clay, sandy, or chalky, and whether it is managed or not. Using a woodland field guide – or by asking a knowledgeable adult – list the types of trees, such as oak, ash, and maple, when you go into a woodland.

◀ **Dense woodland**
This deciduous woodland in the eastern USA has a variety of different tree types. A wide range of animals, such as birds, bats, squirrels, and insects live among the branches.

HANDY TIP
Visit a woodland during late spring, summer, or early autumn when animals are most active.

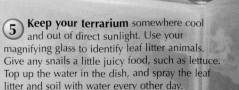

(5) **Keep your terrarium** somewhere cool and out of direct sunlight. Use your magnifying glass to identify leaf litter animals. Give any snails a little juicy food, such as lettuce. Top up the water in the dish, and spray the leaf litter and soil with water every other day.

LEAF LITTER ANIMALS

Here is a checklist of some of the animals you're likely to find. Some feed on decaying plant remains. Others are predators that find their prey as they wriggle through leaf litter.

Centipede ▶
Armed with two poison fangs, centipedes hunt and feed on insects and other small leaf litter animals.

Millipede ▶
With a cylindrical body and lots of legs, millipedes feed by chewing up dead leaves and rotting wood.

Woodlouse ▶
Damp, dark conditions are a woodlouse's favourite, so you won't find them in dry places. Woodlice eat decaying leaves and bits of dead wood.

Beetle ▶
Beetles are very common in leaf litter. Some, such as this ground beetle, hunt for insects, while others eat decaying leaves.

Wolf spider ▶
A daytime hunter, the wolf spider uses its excellent vision and speed to spot and grab any insects that happen to cross its path.

Earwig ▶
With a flat body that's ideal for wriggling through leaf litter, the earwig eats plant material and insects, caught with its pincers.

Springtail ▶
This tiny insect eats dead plants. Its tail, normally tucked under its body, flicks down to push the animal up and away from danger.

Fungus foray

Fungi, such as mushrooms and toadstools,
resemble plants, but live very differently.
They are not green, they don't need
light, they feed on dead or living organisms,
and they reproduce by scattering millions
of microscopic spores. A simple way of
recording the fungi you find is to
make a spore print.

Billions of spores

A type of fungus known as a puffball
(right) can produce billions of spores.
The slightest knock causes spores to puff
out through a hole in the top of the
puffball's cap. If you find a ripe puffball,
tap it and watch its spores escape.

1 **Ask an adult** to cut the
stalk from the mushroom
cap. Look at the underside of
the cap to see the spore-
releasing gills. Put the cap on
a piece of coloured card and
cover it with a bowl to keep
out draughts. Leave overnight.

WHAT YOU WILL NEED

- Mushroom or toadstool
- Coloured card (for
  example, blue, black,
  or light brown)
- Glass or plastic bowl
- Artist's fixative spray
  or hairspray
- Knife

Adult supervision
required. Spray
fixative in a well-
ventilated room.

2 **The next day**, remove
the bowl and carefully lift
the cap. You will see that the
spores have made a print that
matches the gill pattern
of the mushroom.

3 **Carefully spray** the
spore print with fixative to
stop it from being smudged. If
possible, find out what kind of
mushroom or toadstool the
spores came from.

IMPORTANT

Only handle wild fungi if a
knowledgeable adult confirms
that it is safe to do so.
Always wash your hands
after handling fungi.

SAFE OR DANGEROUS?

Some fungi, such as field mushrooms, are good to eat. Others, however, contain poisons. Some of these poisonous species are easily identified, but others can be confused with edible fungi. That is why you should never eat wild fungi unless their identity is confirmed by an expert.

Fly agaric ▶
This toadstool lives near trees, especially birch and spruce. Its bright colour provides a warning that the fly agaric is poisonous.

Puffballs may release more than 5,000 billion spores

NATURE'S RECYCLERS

Many types of fungi, such as bracket fungi, are decomposers. They perform a vital role in nature by disposing of dead plants and animals. A network of slender fungal feeding threads, called hyphae, invade and digest the dead organism, causing it to decay and eventually disappear. This process releases chemicals that are recycled for use by living organisms, such as growing plants.

Bracket fungus ▲
On woodland walks, look out for the shelf-like bracket fungi on the trunks of dead trees. Their hyphae penetrate deep inside the tree, causing it to rot and crumble.

Use a dark card for white spores

4 **Repeat** using different specimens and card colours. Compare the different spore colours and gill patterns.

Dry places

Deserts and other dry places often seem empty and lifeless. But look closely and you'll find that lots of animals and plants use them as their home. Desert animals are mainly active at night when it is cool. Many desert plants survive fierce sunshine and months without rain by storing water in their fleshy stems. You can create a mini desert by planting cacti and other succulents in sandy soil and growing them in a warm place.

WHAT YOU WILL NEED

- Planting tray
- Trowel
- Spoon
- Small watering can
- Gravel
- Compost
- Sand
- A variety of potted cacti and succulent plants, ideally 5–7 specimens

Soil around the roots is loosened before planting

A layer of sand covers the compost

Gravel covers bottom of the planting tray

1 **Cover the bottom** of the planting tray with a shallow layer of gravel. Use the trowel to add compost until the tray is about half full. Place the plant pots around the tray to find the best arrangement.

2 **Dig a small hole** for each plant. Remove the plant from its pot, place it in its hole, and gently press it down. Fill any gaps around the plants with compost. Check that the roots are covered.

3 **Use the spoon** to cover the compost with sand. Press the sand down firmly with the back of the spoon.

AFTER DARK

Do you like to shelter from the Sun on really hot days? Well, so do most desert animals. They either seek out shade or rest in burrows during the day to escape the intense heat. But at night, when temperatures fall, they become active and emerge to search for food.

◄ **Desert jerboa**
Emerging from its burrow at night, this rodent uses its big back feet to hop in search of seeds. Its large eyes are typical of many nocturnal animals.

SNAKE TRACKS

Moving across shifting, painfully hot, desert sand is difficult, but not for sidewinding snakes. They launch their bodies sideways in a series of leaps so that only a small part of their body is in contact with the hot sand for a short amount of time. They leave behind a tell-tale trail of parallel tracks. Look out for them if you visit a desert.

Sidewinding snake ▲
A desert adder from the Namib desert in southern Africa moves across the sand leaving behind its typical sidewinding tracks.

4 **Give your mini desert** a light water and place it in a warm sunny position indoors. Lightly water once every week or two weeks, but never let the soil get too wet. Watch your mini desert plants thrive in their dry, warm surroundings.

Freshwater ponds

Pond wildlife ranges from tiny shrimps, looping leeches, and grazing snails of all sizes, to fish, tadpoles, and an array of insects, not to mention algae, pondweed and other pond plants. Most of you probably know of a pond that you can visit, so here is an ideal nature-ranging opportunity to explore a fascinating habitat.

WHAT YOU WILL NEED

- Dip net with a fine mesh net
- Two plastic containers, such as empty ice-cream tubs
- Small, clear plastic dish
- Clean pipette (dropper)
- Fine paintbrush
- Plastic spoon
- Magnifying glass
- Notebook and pencil
- Field guide to pond life

Always go with an adult to a pond, stream, or river and take care on the banks.

1 **Find a clean**, unpolluted pond. Choose a location where you can approach the water's edge safely. Half-fill both containers with clean water from the pond. Now slowly sweep your dip net through the pond.

2 **Turn the net** inside-out over one of the containers to release any animals or plants you have caught. If you haven't had much luck, try dipping through an area of weeds, as more animals tend to gather here.

IMPORTANT

Always return the animals you have caught to the same part of the pond.

DRAGONFLIES

You can't fail to spot these fantastic insects with their long bodies, large wings, and big eyes. Dragonflies are daytime hunters that prey on other flying insects. Their eggs, laid in ponds, hatch into predatory larvae called nymphs that lurk, well-camouflaged, in mud and vegetation, grabbing passing pond animals with their piercing jaws.

Emerging adult ▶
Dragonfly nymphs live underwater for up to five years, shedding their skin as they grow. Eventually, the nymph climbs out of water and sheds its skin for the last time. Look out for emerging adult dragonflies early on summer mornings.

Acilius beetle larva

Dragonfly nymph

Pond skater skims across pond surface

Beetle larva eats small fish

Hawker nymph

Dragonfly nymph is a predator

(3) **Carefully transfer** specimens, using the spoon or paintbrush, to the clean water of the second container. Make a note of what you have caught. Using the pipette, transfer any tiny organisms to the small plastic dish. Try to identify them with your magnifying glass.

(4) **Compare different parts** of the pond including open water, places with pond plants, and the bottom of the pond. You should find that the numbers and types of animals you find vary from area to area.

POND LIFE

All of these animals are commonly found in ponds, as are dragonflies, beetle larvae, and pond skaters.

◀Greater waterboatman
Also called the backswimmer, because it swims upside-down, this predatory insect moves using its long, oar-like hind legs.

Pond snail ▶
Like other snails, pond snails have a rasping radula (tongue) that they use to feed on algae, decaying plant remains, and pond plants (where they also lay eggs).

◀Freshwater shrimp
With long antennae, and transparent, flattened bodies, freshwater shrimps live among stones and pond weed. They feed on decaying pond matter.

Freshwater leech ▶
Leeches move through a pond using their front and rear suckers. Some feed on other soft-bodied animals, while others eat decaying plants.

Mosquito larvae ▲
Moving jerkily, mosquito larvae are a common sight just below the pond surface. They form rounded pupae from which adult mosquitoes emerge.

Make a small pond

Adding a pond to a garden is a really worthwhile nature-ranger project. It instantly increases your area's biodiversity by adding and attracting lots of new wildlife. Some animals will arrive as "passengers" on pond plants, others will fly, walk, or hop to your newly created attraction.

1 **Mark out** the pond's boundary – a bit bigger than the top of the container – with string. Use the spade to dig a hole the same depth as the container.

Dragonflies may visit your pond and lay their eggs on plants or in water

HANDY TIP

If you can't get any stone slabs for the pond edges, try using some logs or old bricks.

Pond snails stick their eggs to these water lily leaves

AMPHIBIAN VISITORS

Your pond may get a visit from amphibians, such as frogs, toads, or newts. Amphibians spend most of the year on land but return to ponds in the spring to mate and lay their eggs. When tadpoles hatch out, observe the way they develop into fully grown adults.

Frog life cycle ▶
After hatching, tadpoles feed and grow in the pond, and undergo an incredible change in shape – called metamorphosis – to become an adult frog.

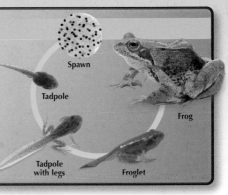

Spawn

Tadpole

Frog

Tadpole with legs

Froglet

(2) **Place the** plastic container into the hole so the top is level with the ground. Fill any gaps with soil.

(3) **Cover the edge** of the pond and the rim of the container with the flat stones or slabs. Place the bricks or large stones in the container to make different levels in the pond.

(4) **Fill the pond** with water. Take the water plants and cover their soil with gravel to stop it floating away. Position the pots in the pond and add free-floating pondweed. Over the next few months, especially in summer, pond insects will take up residence or lay eggs.

WHAT YOU WILL NEED

- Suitable spot in the garden
- Spade
- String
- Large plastic container
- Flat stones or slabs to edge the pond
- Bricks or large stones
- Water plants, such as water lilies, in pots
- Pondweed, such as hornwort or elodea
- Gravel

IMPORTANT

Get permission from an adult before digging holes in the garden!

The seashore

Found where sea and land meet, the seashore is a great place for nature ranging because it is home to an incredible variety of living things. Every seashore – be it sandy, muddy, shingle, or rocky – is a place of constant change where living things have to cope with the tide going in and out twice a day. One way of investigating the wildlife on seashores is to make a shell showcase. This enables you to identify seashore residents by the shells they used to live in.

1 **Visit a beach**. Look for empty shells on rocks and sand, and in pools. Pick the best of each type, and take them home in a bag.

2 **Wash the shells** in cold water to remove traces of sand, seaweed or small animals. Put them on some kitchen paper, with open surfaces down so that water can drain out. Leave them to dry.

3 **Now make** a simple showcase to display and identify the shells you have collected. First of all, take a sheet of cardboard and mark out a rectangle approximately 40 cm x 30 cm (16 in x 12 in).

4 **Draw a margin** 2.5 cm (1 in) wide around the rectangle. Snip the corners with scissors, then fold up the margin to make four sides. Secure these with tape to keep them upright and form a shallow box.

Dune plants ▲
The roots of this marram grass stabilize dunes by binding sand grains together. Spiky stems trap blown sand, so the dunes grow higher.

SAND DUNES

Visit many sandy beaches and you will see sand dunes lying parallel to the shoreline along the landward side of the beach. Dunes form over many years when sand, carried from the beach by the wind, settles to form ripples, then larger ridges, and finally dunes. Sand dunes are really important because they protect land behind the beach from wind and waves. They also provide a habitat for mammals, birds, lizards, and insects, as well as tough plants that can tolerate the harsh, dry, salty conditions.

UNDER THE SURFACE

At low tide, most seashores appear lifeless. But just under the surface there are millions of animals, including marine worms, molluscs, and crustaceans. These creatures become active when the beach is under water. Look out for wading birds patrolling beaches at low tide. They'll be probing with their beaks for juicy prey.

◀ **American avocet**
This wader sweeps its upcurved beak from side to side through watery mud or shallow water to locate worms and crustaceans.

5 **From another** cardboard sheet, cut out eight strips 2.5 cm (1 in) wide – four the same length as the box, and four the same width. Use the strips to divide the box into 25 sections. Tape them in place.

6 **Arrange your** shell collection in the showcase. If you can, use the seashore guide to identify each shell. Add a label to its compartment showing its name, and when and where you found it.

IMPORTANT

Only collect shells that are empty. Don't be tempted to collect shells that still contain living animals as they will die very quickly, rot, and smell.

Rockpools

If you visit a rocky shore, spend some time looking in rockpools. They are great places for watching wildlife because you can see a range of creatures in one place, such as sea anemones, shrimps, starfish, sponges, crabs, and fish – and the occupants are unable to swim away. But one of the problems of looking in rockpools is that sunlight is reflected from the pool's surface, making it difficult to see into the water. To get round this, you can make a rockpool viewer. This will give you a clear view of the teeming life in a rockpool.

Circle drawn on the perspex sheet

1 **Put one end** of the plastic pipe on the perspex. Draw around it using the felt-tip pen to get the right size for the viewer's "window".

2 **Ask an adult** to use the hacksaw to cut carefully around the circle you have just drawn.

A layer of waterproof sealant

3 **Put some** sealant around one end of the plastic pipe. Carefully place the perspex disc on top to make a window. Let the sealant set, then check the window is waterproof in a water-filled sink.

ROCKY SHORE

Most rocky shores provide shelter for a wide variety of seaweeds and marine animals. But life on the rocks can be tough. Twice each day, when the tide comes in, the rocky shore and its wildlife is battered by the waves. Then, when the tide goes out, the animals and seaweeds – whether or not in rockpools – are exposed to the harsh effects of the Sun and wind.

Waves batter a rocky shore in California, USA

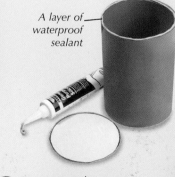

WHAT YOU WILL NEED

- Drainpipe or other large diameter plastic pipe 30–40 cm (12–16 in) long
- Perspex sheet
- Felt-tip pen
- Hacksaw
- Waterproof sealant
- Seashore field guide

⚠ Ask an adult to cut the perspex.

SEA ANEMONES

They may look like plants, but sea anemones are actually flesh-eating animals. Any small creature that ventures near the anemone's tentacles is stung by a battery of stinging cells, paralysed, and pulled into its mouth. Try feeding an anemone by gently brushing a small piece of meat across its tentacles. Wear rubber gloves in case it's a species that can sting you!

Feeding an anemone ▶
The anemone detects chemicals released by the meat, then extends its tentacles to grab its "prey".

④ Kneel down next to a rockpool and push the window end of the viewer into the water. Look through the window and try to identify the animals you spot.

IMPORTANT
Visit a rocky shore only when accompanied by an adult. Check the time of high tide so that you are not cut off when the tide comes in.

Helping wildlife

It's fun to explore nature and discover its fascinating secrets, but don't take the natural world for granted. As the human population increases and takes up more space, and we consume ever more resources, many types of animals and plants are finding survival more and more difficult. Scientists and nature lovers do their best to help them survive, and there are ways in which you can help, too. A good start is to encourage animals to visit your garden, or you can join an organization that conserves (saves) wildlife.

Feeding the birds

Winter can be a tough time for many small birds, so putting up a feeder can help them survive the cold. Seeds give birds, such as these house sparrows, a real energy boost.

CONSERVATION

Released into the wild ▲
Soaring high in the sky, this California condor was released in the Grand Canyon, Arizona, USA, by conservationists who have rescued these American vultures from extinction.

Many animals and plants world-wide are now threatened with extinction. Fortunately, some of these threatened species are being saved by conservation. Take the California condor, America's biggest bird and one of the world's most endangered species. Numbers of the birds fell to just 25 in the 1980s. But scientists started breeding the birds in captivity. Now there are more than 150 birds released into the wild. Try to find out more about conservation organizations and how you can help them.

LESS LITTER

Two easy ways to help wildlife are, firstly, not to leave litter, and, secondly, to encourage your family to recycle packaging, such as cardboard, as much as possible. Litter and garbage, especially plastic, kill many animals every day.

◀ **Shrouded in plastic**
This plastic sheet could harm or kill the deer by preventing it from feeding.

Bug boxes
Put a bug box, such as the one shown here, in your garden. In summer, it provides a place for solitary bees to lay their eggs. In winter, it will provide shelter for helpful, pest-eating ladybirds and lacewings.

Insect-attracting plants
Summer wouldn't be the same without buzzing bees and fluttering butterflies. But both types of insects will only visit if there are nectar-providing flowers to feed on, so plant insect-attracting plants, such as buddleia and snapdragons.

Peacock butterfly feeds on the buddleia flowers

WHAT YOU CAN DO

- Check the internet or phone directory for local nature clubs.
- Visit a natural history museum if there is one near you.
- Take a trip to a zoo or botanical garden to see a wide range of living things.
- Tell your friends about being a nature ranger so they can join in.

Glossary

Backbone A flexible chain of bones called vertebrae that provides the central axis of the skeleton of vertebrate animals.

Biodiversity The variety of species of living things in a particular area.

Biology The study of living things. Scientists who study biology are called biologists.

Cacti (singular cactus) A group of plants that are adapted to dry conditions by having succulent water-storing stems.

Camouflage A disguise in the form of coloration or body shape that enables an animal to blend in with its surroundings.

Carnivores Animals, such as wolves, whose diet consists mainly or entirely of meat.

Chlorophyll Green pigment that colours plants and traps the Sun's energy during photosynthesis.

Circumference The distance round a circular object.

Cold-blooded Describes an animal, such as a lizard, whose body temperature varies with that of its surroundings.

Conifers Plants, mostly tall forest trees, that produce their seeds in cones.

Conservation The protection of endangered wildlife and habitats.

Deciduous Describes trees, such as oak and maple, that shed their leaves at a certain time of year, often in the autumn.

Decomposers Living things, such as bacteria or fungi, that feed on, and break down, dead plants and animals.

Defecate To pass waste in the form of faeces out of an animal's body.

Dicots Short for dicotyledons, a group of flowering plants that has net-veined leaves and flower parts arranged in fours or fives.

Dormant Describes a living thing that is alive but totally inactive.

Evaporation The change of a liquid, such as water, into a gas at a temperature below its boiling point.

Evergreen Describes trees, such as pine and holly, that shed and replace their leaves constantly, so are always in leaf.

Extinction The permanent disappearance of a species of living thing.

Fruit A structure produced by flowering plants that contains and protects seeds.

Germination The start of growth of a seed into a seedling.

Ginkgo A type of tree that is the sole surviving member of an ancient group of seed-producing, non-flowering plants.

Herbivores Animals, such as deer, that feed exclusively on plants.

Hyphae (singular hypha) The tiny filaments or threads that make up a fungus, and through which it feeds.

Invertebrate A general term for any animal, such as a butterfly, sea anemone, garden snail, or earthworm, without a backbone.

Landward Lying towards the land, away from water.

Leaf litter Decaying leaves and other plant material lying on top of soil.

Mammal A warm-blooded animal, such as a mouse, with fur, that feeds its young on milk.

Micro-organism A tiny living thing, such as a bacterium, too small to be seen without a microscope.

Migration The regular movement, at a certain time of year, by animals from one location to another in order to find food or to breed.

Monocots Short for monocotyledons, a group of flowering plants with parallel-veined leaves and flower parts arranged in threes or multiples of three.

Mustelids Group of mammals that includes weasels, polecats, otters, and badgers.

Naturalist A person who is interested in, and studies, nature.

Nectar A sweet liquid produced by flowers to attract pollinating animals.

Nocturnal Describes an animal that is active at night.

Nutrient A substance taken in by a living thing for use in growth, repair, or supplying energy.

Omnivores Animals, such as bears, whose diet consists of a mixture of meat and plants.

Organism A living thing.

Oxygen A gas found in air that is taken in by living things to release energy from food.

Photosynthesis The process by which plants make food from simple substances using sunlight energy.

Pollination The transfer of pollen from the male part of a flower to the female part of the same or a different flower.

Pollutant A harmful substance or material that, when released into the living world, disrupts its natural balance.

Predator An animal that catches, kills, and eats other animals.

Reproduction The production of offspring by living things.

Rodents A large group of small to medium-sized mammals with gnawing teeth that includes rats, squirrels, and beavers.

Root The part of a plant that anchors it in soil, and takes in water and nutrients.

Runner A stem that grows along the ground from a "parent" plant and forms new independent plants.

Seed A structure containing an embryo (baby) plant and its food store, produced by plants when they reproduce.

Shoot The part of a plant, consisting of stem and leaves, that grows above ground towards the light.

Skeleton A framework made of bone or other material that supports an animal's body and enables it to move.

Species A group of living things, such as Scots pines or Virginia opossums, whose members breed only with their own kind.

Spore A tiny package of cells released by fungi, mosses, and ferns when they reproduce.

Succulents Plants, such as cacti and spurges, that survive in dry places by storing water in stems or leaves.

Tapetum The tapetum lucidum is a reflecting layer in the eyes of certain nocturnal animals that enhances night vision.

Tendril A thread-like structure that coils round anything it touches, used by certain plants for support.

Terrarium An enclosure, such as an empty fish tank, for keeping land animals and/or plants.

Territory An area, defended by an animal, which provides food, shelter, and a safe place to bring up offspring.

Transpiration The loss of water vapour by evaporation from a plant's leaves.

Tree A large, woody plant with a single main stem (trunk).

Tropical rainforest A forest that grows near the equator and is wet and warm all year round.

Vertebrate The general term for an animal, such as a fish, frog, snake, sparrow, or lion, that has a backbone.

Warm-blooded Describes an animal, such as a mammal, whose body temperature is controlled regardless of external conditions.

Water vapour A form of water found in the air, which condenses to form water droplets in clouds and rain.

Index

The author and DK would like to thank David Burnie for work on the initial stages of this book.

Model Jack Williams
Index Hilary Bird

The publisher would like to thank the following for their kind permission to reproduce their photographs:

a=above; b=below; c=centre; l=left; r=right; t=top.
Front flap, sponges: Science Photo Library/ Alexis Rosenfeld, kingfishers: naturepl.com/ Philippe Clement, woodpeckers: © Jane Burton/Dorling Kindersley, herons: © Kim Taylor/Dorling Kindersley, marsupials: naturepl.com/Tom Vezo. Back flap, moulds: Science Photo Library/Vaughan Fleming; 4t naturepl.com/Juan Manuel Borrero, c Warren Photographic, b NASA; 5t FLPA/Minden Pictures/Frans Lanting, b Corbis/Galen Rowell; 7b naturepl.com/David Kjaer; 8–9 Ardea, London Ltd/M. Watson; 9tl naturepl. com/Jose P. Ruiz; 11tl Oxford Scientific Films/ David M. Dennis; 14–15 FLPA/Martin B. Withers; 14bl Mike Jordan NEZS (Chester

Zoo); 15tl naturepl.com/George McCarthy, tr NHPA/Mike Lane, ct FLPA/Derek Middleton, cb FLPA/Maurice Nimmo, br Corbis/FLPA/ Michael Callan; 17tl FLPA/Silvestris Fotoservice, tr Oxford Scientific/Richard Packwood; 18tl Corbis/Marko Modic, tr Warren Photographic; 19c Warren Photographic; 21c FLPA/S. Charlie Brown, br Oxford Scientific/Roland Mayr; 22t FLPA/ Mitsuhiko Imamori, bl courtesy of the Natural History Museum, London; 23tl Alamy/Andrew Darrington, tr courtesy of the Natural History Museum, London, c FLPA/Tim Fitzharris, bc FLPA/Robert Canis, br naturepl.com/Adrian Davies; 24lc NHPA/Daniel Heuclin; 25t FLPA/Leonard Lee Rue; 26-27 Corbis/Rose Hartman; 26bl Corbis/Martin Harvey; 27tl FLPA/Minden Pictures/Tui De Roy, tr naturepl. com/Mike Wilkes, c Still Pictures/Paul Springett; 28-29 Corbis/William Gottlieb; 28c Robert Goodden/www.wwb.co.uk, bl Corbis/ Mark L. Stephenson, br Alamy/Photofusion Picture Library/Stan Gamester; 29bl naturepl. com/John Downer, bc Getty Images/Stone/ John Lund, br Getty Images/National Geographic/Jim & Jamie Dutcher; 33bc Stephen Oliver (c) Dorling Kindersley; 35l Stephen Oliver (c) Dorling Kindersley; 36b

Alamy/Genevieve Vallee; 37r FLPA/Minden Pictures/Frans Lanting; 40t Alamy/Rosey Pajak, br Oxford Scientific/IFA-Bilderteam GMBH; 41l Alamy/Alan Mather, tr Alamy/ Renee Morris, br naturepl.com/Rolf Nussbaumer; 43tl FLPA/S&D&K Maslowski, cr Science Photo Library/Lynwood Chase, br Science Photo Library/David Nanuk; 44cl Corbis/David Muench, bl Corbis/George H. H. Huey; 45tl NHPA/George Bernard; 48bl Ardea, London/John Mason, br Alamy/The Garden Picture Library/John Glover; 50bl Howard Rice (c) Dorling Kindersley; 51tr Stephen Oliver (c) Dorling Kindersley; 55tl naturepl.com/AFLO, br NHPA/N.A. Callow; 58b FLPA/Arthur Christiansen; 59br Ardea, London/M. Watson; 60l Powerstock/age fotostock; 61tl Ardea, London/Geoff Trinder; 64bl NHPA/Laurie Campbell; 65tl Ardea, London/B. Moose Peterson; 66l Alamy/Danita Delimont; 67b Oxford Scientific/Claude Steelman; 68t FLPA/Foto Natura/Flip de Nooyer, b NHPA/Daniel Heuclin; 69tr Oxford Scientific/Lon E. Lauber, cr www. wildlifeworld.co.uk, br NHPA/Stephen Dalton

All other images © Dorling Kindersley
www.dkimages.com